MIDNIGHT THOUGHTS

Shaun M. Wilkinson

I0164063

Table of Contents

To Maw and Paw Aime, for your encouragement and unyielding support.

To Mom and Pops, for raising me right.

To Isabella, Christian and Esteban, love with all your hearts, play hard, and never grow up.

And to Cecilia, for always supporting me and continuing to travel along this crazy road we call life; my love and my partner in crime.

MIDNIGHT THOUGHTS

#1

The clock reads midnight
Still I lay here, wide awake-
Sleep does not exist

#2

Bullet pierces bone
Pears roll along the pavement-
Screams ignite the air

#3

Cool breeze
Sunlight breaks through-
Grey clouds bring the storm

#4

Downpour
From chaos comes new life-
Raging water

#5

Rent money drops
Pulse races as the reels spin-
An empty hopper

#6

Time to play ball
A hotdog vendor calls out-
Smell of peanuts

#7

Walk tall in the world
Through His love-
Prostrate

#8

Long, hollow breath
Heartbeat flutter-
Cold cuts the skin

#9

Scorching blast
Lungs filling with dust-
Shamal

#10

Eyes open, glance
Momentary contact-
Warm cheeks

#11

Brown pierces
Staring into the soul-
Find a way in

#12

The cursor taunts me
Exposing failure with each blink
Who the fuck am I?

#13

A shadow flaps its wings
Glide under the surface-
Bird of the sea

#14

Wield a knife
Freedom's ultimate death-
Flailing beauty

#15

A pull from the shore
Try to keep your footing-
Sand giving way

#16

Head down, walking
Searching in vain-
The treasure is around him

#17

Lou'siana moon
Fog hugs the water–
Beasts lie in wait

#18

Sick or haunted
Feel my breath–
Chills the bones

#19

Engine down
Red drifts across Eurus's sky–
Fury on the water

#20

Jackhammer
Pound to the bone–
Set me free

#21

Calm precedes the storm
Stoic-
The raving madman

#22

Mirrors hung along the walls
Who holds the key to my despair?
Damn, you!

#23

Freight train bare down
Land Run in sight-
Ripping hope from the boxcar

#24

Slicing at my sanity
Spread among the hot coals-
Shattered glass

#25

Shallow breeze
Swallow the cold-
Warmth ushers new life

#26

I walk in sunlight
Begging for darkness-
It denies me

#27

Conjure the past
Solitary breath-
It all burned down

#28

Darkness abound
In the recess of my heart–
Nightmares

The End

Interconnected
Disconnection
Strangled by the wires-
Digital waves
Sexually depraved
Desiring no affection-
Masturbation
Love is lust
Ejaculating dust-
In the end we all stare
through blood drenched memories

About The Author

Shaun M. Wilkinson (born 1983) spent the majority of his childhood in St. Amant, Louisiana. He is a United States Army combat veteran, amateur sports tweeter, karaoke master, horror fanatic, and author of the four books of poetry.

Shaun currently resides in Texas with his wife and children.

www.ingramcontent.com/pod-product-compliance
Lightning Source LLC
Chambersburg PA
CBHW020446030426
42337CB00014B/1426